A

Celebration

of

Marriage

A Celebration of Marriage

Hopes and Realities

Edith Schaeffer

A Raven's Ridge Book

Baker Books

A Division of Baker Book House Co.
Grand Rapids, Michigan 49516

Scripture references not otherwise identified are based on the King James Version of the Bible.

Scripture references identified NIV are from the HOLY BIBLE, NEW INTERNATIONAL VERSION®. NIV®. Copyright © 1973, 1978, 1984 by International Bible Society. Used by permission of Zondervan Publishing House. All rights reserved.

Excerpts from *The Art of Life* by Edith Schaeffer is © by Crossway Books, Westchester, Illinois. Used by permission.

Except for new material written by Edith Schaeffer expressly for this work, other excerpts have been taken from the following Baker Book House/Raven's Ridge books: *Affliction*, *What Is a Family?*, *The Tapestry*, *Forever Music* and *Ten Things Parents Must Teach Their Children (And Learn for Themselves)*.

ISBN 0-8010-8354-0

Printed in the United States of America

Contents

Searching for reasons to express love, thinking about them and formulating appreciation into words takes time. "Time" can be so completely absorbed by dwelling on each other's mistakes that there is never time to increase love.

CHAPTER ONE

Shared Thoughts and a Cup of Tea

*A*re you in that uncertain, hesitant period of your life wondering whether this is the one you want to spend the rest of your life with?

Are you soon to be married, or newly wed?

Or have you been married for awhile and desire renewed perspective on the nature and purpose of marriage?

If so, go fix a cup of tea and find a comfortable reading place. I'd like to talk with you. As we sit and talk about marriage, with new leaves coming on the spring trees, buds appearing on the bushes, birds singing their diverse songs or with snow covering those same trees with white magic, the sun bringing out the individual flakes to look like diamonds scattered on white velvet, we need to keep some facts in mind.

For one, remember that ever since the fall there is no perfect person, no perfect combination of persons, no perfect husbands, no perfect wives, no perfect fathers and mothers, no perfect families, no perfect marriage.

Not only are we imperfect, but each of us is unique. There are no clones. We are complex, alive both spiritually and physically. Unlike statues of marble which change very slowly through the years, we are growing and changing all the time. We are continually improving or deteriorating in understanding, knowledge and skills, both spiritually, morally and intellectually.

As we grow and change, we affect others. We can affect their ideas, behavior and accomplishments. We can inspire and encourage one another in all areas—the arts, music, literature, painting, sculpting, film making, gardening . . . or we can cast gloom and discouragement.

There are no carbon copies of any situation . . . nor of any relationship. We can't inspect our relationships like some worker at a factory, and discard them if they don't meet the factory standard.

In *A Celebration of Marriage,* I share my story—the story of two imperfect human beings creating a marriage together. This anthology of writings, both old and new, chronicles my almost forty-nine years of marriage to Francis Schaeffer, and the lessons learned along the way. As we sip our tea, and I share my thoughts, I hope you are encouraged and inspired to take seriously and handle thoughtfully this very important human relationship—marriage.

CHAPTER TWO

Edith and Francis Meet

It was June 26, 1932, after graduation, that I went to the Young People's meeting as usual on Sunday night. The topic for the night had been selected by the "leader," Ed Broom. The fact that he had formerly been a member of the Presbyterian Church and of this society, but had left to join the Unitarian Church seemed to make no difference to anyone as to his being the leader. His topic was "How I know that Jesus is not the Son of God, and how I know that the Bible is not the Word of God." I sat down and began to fume inside. As I listened, my reaction was to jot down things in my head to use in a rebuttal —things I had gathered from lectures about the original manuscripts that I felt might help people who were listening, even if they did nothing to convince Ed Broom. As soon as he had finished I jumped up to my feet and started to open my mouth . . . when I heard another voice, a boy's voice, quietly begin to talk. I slid back into my seat and listened, startled.

"You all may think what I am going to say is influenced by my having sat all this year under a Bible teacher at Hampden Sydney College whom you would term 'old-fashioned.' He has taught the Bible to be the Word of God, and I do believe that too. I want to say that I know Jesus is the Son of God, and He is also my Savior, and has changed my life. I've been away all year, and this is the first time any of you has seen me since college, but although I can't answer all the things Ed has said, I want you to know just where I stand."

"Who is that?" I whispered to Ellie Fell beside me. "I didn't know there was a real believing Christian in this church. . . ." "That," said Ellie in a hoarse whisper, "is Fran Schaeffer, and his parents have been real mean to him because they don't want him to be a pastor." My mind resolved to somehow comfort "the poor boy," but I then jumped up to say what I had been going to say.

My "say" was made up of some quotes from Dr. Machen and Dr. Robert D. Wilson, and it gave that type of apologetic for the truth of the Bible which I had heard in lectures and read. Then I sat down. While I was speaking, Fran whispered to Dick, the fellow sitting next to him, "Who on earth is that girl? I didn't know anyone in this church knew that kind of thing." Dick's reply was, "That is Edith Seville, and she has just moved here from Toronto, Canada. Her parents used to be missionaries in China."

As the last hymn was sung, and the benediction "May the Lord watch between me and thee while we are absent one from another" was mumbled, the usual hubbub occurred of everyone trying to get out quickly to the "real" evening, at someone's home. I saw Dick and Fran

Schaeffer pushing through people, coming in my direction. Suddenly Dick was saying, "Edith, I want to introduce you to Fran Schaeffer. Fran, this is Edith Seville." (People introduced people in those days!) Fran's next words were, "May I take you home?" I replied, "I'm sorry, but I already have a date." Whereupon Fran flatly urged, "Break it." Desire to communicate with someone who really believed and had courage to say so overcame my natural inclination not to break a promised date, although it was only to go to Ellie's house. So I said, "Well . . . yes, I guess I will." We walked out to the sidewalk followed by Dick and a couple of others who were giving instructions as to how to get to Ellie's and making fun of Fran for not being able to find his keys. (Fran always panicked about finding a key at the time he needed it!) And soon we were off.

Our conversation was about serious things of Christianity—not just its defense, but the wonder of all we believe. However, we had met "on the battlefield," and for almost forty-nine years we stood together on two sides of the room, so to speak, but on the same side of the issues in a diversity of places and in the midst of an ongoing history.

Just as you are not to be unfaithful to God, you are not to be unfaithful to your mate. The oneness is a daily, constant picture throughout all history of the oneness between God and His people.

CHAPTER THREE

Becoming One

There are three circles of oneness that human beings have been given the capacity to have. These three circles are important to bear in mind not only during the "falling in love" stage prior to marriage, but throughout married life. Like the tuning of a fine piano, each circle of possible oneness needs ongoing attention.

The first circle represents all the eligible Christians in the world. The Bible makes it clear that one must be equally yoked with another Christian in the marriage relationship. However among the eligible Christians there are many you could not feel akin to. In fact there are many Christians who would make you feel uncomfortable and scratchy. It is important to find someone you can pray with, read and discuss Scripture with.

The second circle represents the eligible Christians in the world who have similar interests and preferences in food, books, music, skiing, swimming or tennis, old or new houses, cities or country, mountain vacations or vacations by the sea, boats or art museums, playing chess or tiddlywinks. . . .

The third circle represents the physical attraction, which sometimes is unexplainable, something like a spark or a flash of lightning, an alluring pull of what seems like magnetism. The fascination of such attraction is meant for one purpose: "Therefore shall a man leave his father and his mother and shall cleave to his wife; and the two shall become one flesh."

As you are considering marriage, you should seek to find someone with as much balance in these three circles as possible. The area where all three circles overlap to form a small triangle includes a small number of possible people who would make a suitable marriage partner. There are more people represented in the area where just two circles cross, but this won't do for marriage.

Once the vows are made, the husband and wife must determine to spend time, work, imagination and creativity to increase the oneness through the years.

Someone wrote me recently and told me of a married man who spent at least one full day per week, often more, with a single woman. Though they did not have a physical relationship, they took walks together, listened to music together and shared ideas about art, literature and so on. "What about it?" the writer of the letter asked. My thoughts immediately jumped to the three circles. I replied, "To give time developing a relationship with a person who has a great deal in common in the spiritual and intellectual areas, is to steal time, imagination and creativity away from one's spouse. Single people can spend as much time together as they want, but a marriage, especially one having problems, needs all the creativity, imagination, work and time that can be found.

Would I call this man's relationship with the single woman adultery? No, I wouldn't use that word, but I do feel that it is robbing his marriage of the creative work that needs to be constantly given. It is like turning in a half-finished art project, sculpture or musical score that one has been paid to do. It's like using time and ideas to benefit a rival firm.

It is important to examine the three circles of oneness frequently throughout the years of marriage, not in order to criticize one's mate, but to help recognize where one is stealing time, creativity and originality from the marriage relationship. There must be a willingness to work for a lifetime at growing closer, getting rid of hindrances and developing matching interests.

Understanding does not come immediately and completely. Understanding usually takes some amount of time, but the first requirement of understanding is hearing — listening and paying attention to the content of what is being said.

CHAPTER FOUR

Engaged

*F*ran and I met in June, 1932. It was New Year's Eve afternoon at the end of that year, that Fran said "good-bye" to me. He had decided he was growing too fond of me, and that we'd better break up the relationship because probably the Lord wanted him to go where no woman could follow. (I'm not sure just what he visualized that place to be like, nor where it might be.) And with promises to pray for each other, we parted before supper and he went off to his home. We seriously parted . . . "forever"?

My tomato soup had extra salt water in it that night, and my father gruffly remarked, "Of course, no one would tell me what this is all about," and mother patted my shoulder! As they went off for a church meeting, the phone rang for me, and it was a *Saturday Evening Post* cover artist wanting me to go with him to some girl's home with a group of others to listen to records "while the New Year comes in." Since I had still been dating all through that first semester of school, and since I was not going to ever see Fran again, I thought I might as well be sorrowful in the midst of people, rather than all alone. However, as I was getting dressed, the phone rang again, and this time it was Fran. "I've been so miserable since I left you. I know now I can't live without you. Please can I come down for a half hour?" . . . He had been gone a total of two hours! I said, "Yes, of course," and felt relieved that it would only be a half hour, since that wouldn't make too embarrassing a change in the evening! It was during that half hour that Fran asked if I would "wait" for him. It wasn't exactly a proposal, but of course it was! He sealed my answer with a kiss, and then went off to see the New Year in with his parents because he had promised them he would be right back.

When the artist came and we started to drive off, I announced, "Oh, by the way, in between your call and now, I've just more or less gotten engaged. I thought I should tell you!" It sounded pretty ridiculous, but that was exactly the way it was. This was my last date with anyone else. I became a curiosity to the girls at school, not going to the school dances, always being "alone" and in their eyes "wasting" my freedom and my youth and my college life. I was doing an unheard-of thing . . . even if I had had a big diamond to flash at them, which I didn't.

There are so many periods of "waiting" in life that make time seem long, while the rest of life flies! There is waiting to finish school, waiting for exam results, waiting for the wedding day to arrive, and waiting for the baby to take nine months to grow; there is waiting for a long illness to "break" and signs of recovery to be real; there is the waiting for that event all Christians most urgently desire (at least in most periods of their lives)—for Christ to return and restore the fallen world, giving us our new bodies to be His Bride, with only glory ahead and no waiting left. That will be a fulfillment with no shadow of disappointment to which the word "perfection" really applies!

If you are all ready to be envious of perfection in our lives—Fran's and mine, you can stop holding your breath, because there are no perfect people, no perfect relationships, no perfect marriages, no perfect work, no perfect children, no perfect families, no perfect periods of time, and there is no perfect formula for how to have perfection! "But," you may say, "he wrote and told you how perfect you were, and you wrote and told him he had no faults, and you went on and on about it for all that time. . . ." Yes. And we felt very strongly that we could find no flaw in each other. But we were to come to discover what those flaws were and that we were going to live with the flaws, which would become a part of our history, day by day. Never forget, that if you insist on "perfection or nothing" in the area of love or happiness, or any area of human relationship, you will have nothing. So we were going to have some "bumps" discovering realities and sorting out values through the years.

Love will grow as reasons for love are discovered. thought about. dwelt upon in the mind. expressed verbally and remembered. As time goes on. the memory will become rich with increasing vividness and warmth.

CHAPTER FIVE

Understanding Love

Love without reason is sometimes pictured as a meeting of personalities in some mystical blending of baseless emotion. The intellect is put on the other side of a high gray stone wall—where a chilly, dull atmosphere is contrasted to the riot of colored flowers and warm sun-drenched grasses on the "emotion" side of the dividing wall. One is given an impression of needing to make a choice between "mind" and "heart," as if to choose one is to deny the other. "Love, feel, experience. Don't ask, don't question, don't use your mind. Just let yourself go. Come away from the harsh use of logic," shout some who think the wall separating emotion and intellect is rigid and never to be crossed. Love is thought of as so delicate a wisp of cloud that it will be blown away by any wind of verbalized reason.

Is this true? What about human love which, though limited and imperfect, grows through verbalization and deepening understanding.

Dwelling in one's mind on logical reasons for love does not diminish the feelings of love, but increases them. Making new discoveries of qualities in the other person's character, through recent things he or she has done, gives increased reality in the area of knowing the person. Verbalizing these discoveries fixes in the memory some of the reasons that should logically increase love. Love will grow as reasons for love are discovered, thought about, dwelt upon in the mind, expressed verbally and remembered. As time goes on, the memory will become rich with increasing vividness and warmth in storing up facts and reasons behind the increase of love.

How foolish we are in human relationships when we continually dwell upon each other's weaknesses and mistakes. How easily love is squashed and the fire dimmed with a dash of cold water, when the sensitive deed, the proffered rose, the cup of tea, or the concert tickets are ignored, and instead a stream of criticism blasts the air with "Why did you forget to mail the letter?"—"Why did you drop that dish?"— "Why have you brought mud in on your feet?"—"Why didn't you tell me first?" The lack of appreciation certainly hurts the person being screamed at. But the one doing the screaming is losing the possibility of experiencing the growing love that would have taken place had the mind been filled with the obvious and very logical reason for expressing love— and either waiting for a quiet moment to discuss whatever really needed discussing or putting aside the criticism altogether.

Searching for reasons to express love, thinking about them and formulating appreciation into words takes time. "Time" can be so completely absorbed by dwelling on each other's mistakes that there is never time to increase love. The mind needs to be involved in blending the whole person into a reality of growth in the areas of feeling. Emotion needs a base if it is to be a solid, continuing experience. We can help ourselves to have a continuity in our life relationships when we come to recognize that there is no wall between intellect, mind, logical understanding—and the warmth of growing love.

Love isn't just happiness in ideal situations with everything going according to daydreams of married life. Love has work to do! Love takes imagination and the balance of putting first things first.

CHAPTER SIX

The Wedding

July 6, 1935, was one of those hot muggy Philadelphia summer days with the temperature in the nineties and the humidity the same. Strains of Mendelssohn from the church organ drifted out the door of the little United Presbyterian Church on Wayne Avenue in Germantown. People in the pews temporarily stopped their hand-manipulated fans and moved over a bit, as room had to be made for latecomers. Some of those who had been sitting made movements away from the back of the pew as perspiration seemed to glue their clothing to the wood. The wild flowers looked fresh in spite of a few drooping heads, and those who had picked them that morning smiled with satisfaction at each other. It was precisely four o'clock, and a whole new piece of history was beginning. Francis August Schaeffer, born in 1912 right there in Germantown, and Edith Rachel Seville, born in 1914 in Wenchow, Chekiang Province, China, were about to become the first generation of a new family!

The father of the bride waited at the front with the bridegroom, watching his youngest daughter come forward to be given away to become, with the bridegroom, a separate family. He quietly prayed he wouldn't be overcome with emotion as he asked the questions as officiating pastor. The organ music played an accompaniment to his mixed feelings of sadness and joy as this would be a new beginning for him too. The mother of the bride and the mother of the bridegroom leaned out into the aisle a bit, one on one side, the other on the opposite, each thinking her separate thoughts set to the music coursing through her brain—thoughts to be remembered the next time she heard the same bars played again.

The bride herself walked properly . . . step . . . step . . . step . . . with practiced timing and natural grace, not too rapidly, trying to walk as if alone and yet smoothly blending with the professor's more jerky steps. The overwhelming realization hit her that this flower-strewn walk was a farewell walk, one saying good-bye to the family togetherness with her parents in the known pattern, and a titanic step into the beginning of a future life and family with a new pattern. That sudden recognition made it necessary to take her eyes away from her mother's smiling encouragement, and to pin them unswervingly on the bridegroom's face. "Hello," not "good-bye," was all her emotions could stand at that moment. There stood her groom looking at her as if no one else existed in the room, almost as if he wished they'd leave.

No one could "hear" the ideas racing through minds that day in 1935. Silence filled the church as the soloist's voice stopped its outpouring of words about "oh perfect love," and Dr. Seville's firm voice began to read words from his little, white leather-covered book:

Dearly beloved, we are assembled here in the presence of God, to join this Man and this Woman in holy marriage; which is instituted of God, regulated by His commandments, blessed by our Lord Jesus Christ, and to be held in honor among all men. Let us therefore reverently remember that God has established and sanctified marriage, for the welfare and happiness of mankind. Our Savior has declared that a man shall forsake his father and mother and cleave unto his wife. By His apostles, He has instructed those who enter into this relation to cherish a mutual esteem and love; to bear with each other's infirmities and weaknesses; to comfort each other in sickness, trouble, and sorrow; in honesty and industry to provide for each other, and for their household, in temporal things; to pray for and encourage each other in the things which pertain to God; and to live together as heirs of the grace of life.

How many were thinking of their own past vows as they listened? To how many were the words a real communication of the reality of lasting marriage. And to how many were the words simply syllables without meaning. The little, white leather book after forty-nine years still has the fine handwriting of Dr. Seville where he wrote in the names.

Francis, wilt thou have this Woman to be thy wife, and wilt thou pledge thy troth to her, in all love and honor, in all duty and service, in all faith and tenderness, to live with her and cherish her, according to the ordinance of God, in the holy bond of marriage.

(And the Man shall answer: "I will.")

Edith, wilt thou have this Man to be thy husband, and wilt thou pledge thy troth to him, in all love and honor, in all duty and service, in all faith and tenderness, to live with him and cherish and obey him, according to the ordinance of God, in the holy bond of marriage.

(And the Woman shall answer: "I will.")

Then the father of the bride, who was now becoming father-in-law of the bridegroom, took the right hand of the bridegroom and the right hand of the bride and placed them together asking for the following vows to be repeated:

I, Francis, take thee, Edith, to be my wedded wife; And I do promise and covenant; Before God and these witnesses; To be thy loving and faithful husband; In plenty and in want; In joy and in sorrow; In sickness and in health; As long as we both shall live.

Loosing hands so that there might be a specific taking again of hands for this declaration:

I, Edith, take thee, Francis, to be my wedded husband; And I do promise and covenant; Before God and these witnesses; To be thy loving and faithful wife; In plenty and in want; In joy and in sorrow; In sickness and in health; As long as we both shall live.

The giving of the ring followed this, and further prayer, as well as the formal declaration that they were now husband and wife, according to the ordinance of God and the law of the Commonwealth of Pennsylvania. The final strong utterance followed:

Whom God hath joined together, let no man put asunder. "Till Death Do Us Part."

"Till death do us part" is a big and important promise; "for better or for worse" is a fantastically realistic promise. A lot of time is being vowed, and a lot of situations are being suggested. This is a set of promises for imperfect people to make to imperfect people in an abnormal world where everything has been spoiled since the fall! "For richer or for poorer" is a reminder of Paul's declaration that he is able to be abased or to abound. This is what we are meant to vow to the Lord as our willingness in serving Him; we will serve Him no matter what—in palaces or in huts, in distressing situations and in beautiful ones, which if He gives we need not be ashamed. So in our marriage declarations we need not whisper but speak so that people can hear us say that we are stepping into a "togetherness," facing an unknown future which neither one can know about ahead of time.

There is a mystical oneness God has made possible in the sexual relationship which belongs not to promiscuousness, but to a continuity in marriage, because it parallels the eternal oneness we have when we are united with the Lord.

CHAPTER SEVEN

The Sexual Relationship

There is a mystical oneness God has made possible in the sexual relationship which belongs not to promiscuousness, but to a continuity in marriage, because it parallels the eternal oneness we have when we are united with the Lord. Once we belong to the Lord it is forever. It is not a casual relationship, and Christians are meant to realize that their precious bodies which will be raised from the dead one day are to have their sexual relationships in the right framework. To make sex the integration point in life, and to seek fulfillment in any way that comes into one's mind or onto one's path is taking that which has been created for one purpose and using it for a very different thing.

Have you ever seen the loving care with which a maker of fine wood furniture gathers wood and seasons it, preparing it for just the right matching of grain in making his chairs and cabinets and tables? Think of someone wanting to warm himself in front of a fire coming and chopping up all that precious oak, walnut, cherry, mahogany, and making a fire in the fireplace as he sits and eats and drinks by the blaze. What a waste!

No illustrations are perfect, but sex, which is a central factor in manipulating human beings today, and a central factor in breaking up marriages in so many parts of the world, is being twisted into that which destroys the Who am I? and the How can I be fulfilled? altogether. It is like the fire made with the valuable and rare wood with its matched grain all ready for something beautiful. It has been misused.

The reasons for not committing sexual sin are listed in 1 Corinthians: "Flee from sexual immorality. All other sins a man commits are outside his body, but he who sins sexually sins against his own body. Do you not know that your body is a temple of the Holy Spirit, who is in you, whom you have received from God? You are not your own; you were bought at a price. Therefore honor God with your body."

The first reason is that it is a sin against your own body which is not made for such use. Second, it is a terrible thing to use your body, which really is lived in by the Holy Spirit, for that which is sinful. Third, you have been bought because Jesus died in your place, so you don't belong to yourself anymore.

There is so very much talk about people owning their own bodies today—especially by women who claim that they have a right not only to do what they want to sexually, but to make their bodies a graveyard for their own children, the relative that is closest to them. For a Christian, all the talk about a "right to my body" is all wrong! Our bodies belong to the One who died so that we can be certain of having transformed bodies that will be perfect for all eternity. They have been paid for by Jesus, and we need to study how we are supposed to use them, and recognize sin and ask forgiveness for what we have done wrong with our bodies.

The seventh chapter of 1 Corinthians offers the remedy for avoiding sexual temptation. "But since there is so much immorality, each man should have his own wife, and each woman her own husband. The husband should fulfill his marital duty to his wife, and likewise the wife to her husband" (7:2).

The way to avoid immorality is the fulfillment of each person's need within the framework of marriage. There is no one-sidedness in what is outlined here; there is a careful admonition which indicates that each one is to care for the other person's needs, rather than fighting for their personal rights. The unselfish regard for the other person means that there are no excuses for withdrawal or denial or coldness in the physical area of marriage. It would be as serious if a wife or husband refused to cook or provide a meal because of not feeling hungry, and at the same time refused to talk during the mealtime and eat with the other one because of feeling hostile. Each day requires working at it, even when it does not flow naturally. It must be a growing-together relationship, so that a wall is being built against the invasion of what Satan will try to throw into your marriage to spoil it.

Read on:

"The wife's body does not belong to her alone but also to her husband. In the same way, the husband's body does not belong to him alone but also to his wife. Do not deprive each other except by mutual consent and for a time, so that you may devote yourselves to prayer."

This is extremely clear. When you say "I do," you have given your body to each other, and selfishness is out. The only proper reason given for depriving the other one of the physical relationship is that time may be had for prayer. And this special time to be taken for prayer is to be a decision by mutual consent. It is a kind of fasting and prayer which is decided on together for some special reason, even as a meal is put aside to spend that time in prayer for some special reason. But it is not right, according to this instruction about the physical side of married life in Corinthians, to say, "No, not tonight, I'm going to pray," and then to go off feeling pious about being more spiritual than the other person.

The next sentence makes it very specific that the person turning away and refusing is involved in any fall that may come because of a temptation. The warning is like the blast of a horn in order to capture attention.

Listen: "Then come together again so that Satan will not tempt you because of your lack of self-control."

This is the last half of verse 5, which says that the only reason for staying apart is for prayer. Notice that the time of prayer is not to be counted on to push away the temptation, but that a practical protection is given in order to foil Satan. The word here is that, "To avoid having your children steal buns from the bakery, have fresh baked buns waiting for them at home after school." It is the same kind of practical warning that if marriage is indeed to help people stay away from immorality, then there should be a responsibility taken by each of the two to fulfill each other's needs as much as possible.

CHAPTER EIGHT

Honeymoon

The Model A Ford was packed and ready for us to go. After the reception all we needed to add was my suitcase. The two boxes of food were in. Food? Oh, yes. We had a romantic idea about what were then called "overnight cabins"—cost, $1.00 a night, or, with hot shower, $1.50—and we were going to take a one-burner electric plate, a small pot and a frying pan, dishes, and groceries. You see, this honeymoon was going to cost zilch! I had stupidly filled a little glass jar with butter. (It was July 6, with the temperature in the nineties and the humidity nearly as high.) The other ridiculous side of my preparation was that I had made a trousseau with little hand-tucked blouses, a white "going-away suit," and dainty things that would have been fine in a luxury hotel and resort.

The first thing we did after waving to the rice-throwing guests was to head toward the country and stop at a drug store on the outskirts of town to cool off with a milk shake. In my elegant white suit I sat on a high stool at the counter sipping my chocolate milk shake; then when swirling around to get off, I found that someone else's milk shake had been spilled on the stool. My skirt was hopelessly stained with chocolate milk, ruined.

"Nothing mattered" . . . but that stained skirt kept going through my mind's eye, with all the carefully hand-whipped seams and Paris-couturier type of work I'd done on it . . . just to sit on a drug store stool? It was a vivid first lesson (though I didn't analyze it or even recognize it as that) of the basic fact of relationships—that people matter more than things! Fran remembers clearly that he felt sorry, but that he felt the magic moment of starting out together was more important than the spoiled skirt. He also remembers that I had started to make a fuss about it, but that I stopped short and didn't mention it again. Stopped in mid-air, so to speak, I had made a decision that was not perfectly kept in our lives together, but which was made time after time. The decision was to stop, try to recognize the total value of what was happening, and make a deliberate choice that the broken, torn, spilled, crushed, burned, scratched, smashed, spoiled thing was not as important as the person, or the moment of history, or the memory.

Fran lugged our wooden boxes and hot plate into the little room, then looked around for a spot for his suitcase and for the new big one father had so proudly bought me. Not much floor or hanging space. The jar of butter was leaking its liquefied fat. The cabbages sat on the little table, along with lettuce and tomatoes. . . . Where to put the hamburger? This was one of the more "expensive" cabins and had a shower . . . but where was I going to "glide glamorously" in my hand-made satin nightgown? . . . from where to where? There wasn't an inch of floor space!

The next noon, as the hamburger cooled and the corn and then the cabbage had their turns to cook, the cabin filled with a mixture of fragrances not exactly resembling subtle French perfumes. I'm afraid I must confess that tears of a sudden wave of homesickness engulfed me. Just about now, I thought, Mother and Dad would be sitting down to their lovely Sunday dinner discussing the wedding, and the morning sermon. It hit me that I had severed myself completely from my former home, and as yet I couldn't see at all what that word was going to mean—"home." Human beings and their emotions are unpredictable, and no one has a carbon copy of anyone else's experiences, but I would say that Fran and I have been very careful to see that our own children, and now our grandchildren and also the "spiritual children" close to us, have at least a few days of special luxury to start their honeymoons. So we feel the odor of cabbages and of dirty dishes being washed in the wash basin have helped a lot of other people get started a bit differently.

If husbands tried to copy in some tiny measure the amazing love Christ has for the church, and if wives respected and desired to please their husbands in a small particle of the way we are meant to please and bring joy to Christ—then there would be no problems!

CHAPTER NINE

Thou Shalt Not Commit Adultery

Two little girls in a Swiss boarding school were discussing what they would do when they grew up. The ten-year-old said firmly, "Well, I'm going to stay married for ten years the first time I get married, then I'll try a lot of different husbands."

A panel of social workers and teachers were discussing on television whether it was a breach of confidence to tell mothers when their little girls of nine were coming to them for contraceptives.

Sweden takes pride that there is no distinction between married couples and couples who live together without being married. All the benefits are the same, including alimony if there is a separation.

A strange rash of marriages has been taking place recently with couples who have lived together as much as eight years suddenly wanting something more in continuity and stability, so they turn to a wedding, with smiling children standing in front as flower girls or ring-bearers. Mother and Daddy are getting married!

In the mishmash of today's standards of right and wrong, many children are being born into an atmosphere that is alien to the Ten Commandments, so alien that to simply state them would have no meaning at all. It's as though they were brought up in a house where all the windows had been broken long before they were born and they look out at the world through a distorted perspective. How could you judge the description someone might give you of what your view would be like seen through crystal-clear glass with no drips of glue and none of the myriad cracks. This isn't true only of children, but many adults have also lost sight of the alternatives to the way everyone around them is living.

The Ten Commandments mean nothing at all to much of the world's population. What is even more depressing is that they mean very little to many who call themselves the people of God. The "cracked and glued together glass" has come to believers' homes too, and the warped view is affecting their judgment as well. They forget that God has made people and that He has made the rules in line with who they are.

One of these rules is the seventh commandment: "You shall not commit adultery."

Adultery is the smashing of a rare and mystical oneness between two people who have become one because of something which God made them to be capable of having together. Read again Genesis 1:27; 2:24, 25:

> So God created man in his own image, in the image of God he created him; male and female he created them. . . . For this reason a man will leave his father and mother and be united to his wife, and they will become one flesh. The man and his wife were both naked, and they felt no shame.

The original reason given for the sexual act in marriage is oneness. This physical oneness is a picture of the believer's spiritual oneness with God. The comparison of our being made to have oneness with a human being and our being made to have oneness spiritually with God is made clear in various parts of the Bible, but one of the clearest is in Ephesians 5:25-33:

> Husbands, love your wives, just as Christ loved the church and gave himself up for her to make her holy, cleansing her by the washing with water through the word, and to present her to himself as a radiant church, without stain or wrinkle or any other blemish, but holy and blameless. In this same way, husbands ought to love their wives as their own bodies. He who loves his wife loves himself. After all, no one ever hated his own body, but he feeds and cares for it, just as Christ does the church—for we are members of his body. For this reason a man will leave his father and mother and be united to his wife, and the two will become one flesh. This is a profound mystery—but I am talking about Christ and the church. However, each one of you also must love his wife as he loves himself, and the wife must respect her husband.

Just as you are not to be unfaithful to God, you are not to be unfaithful to your mate. Faithfulness to God and faithfulness to husband and wife are both meant to be fulfilling. But they will only be fulfilling as we follow the teaching that God has been so careful to give us. If husbands tried to copy in some tiny measure the amazing love Christ has for the church, and if wives respected and desired to please their husbands in a tiny manner, a small particle of the way we are meant to please and bring joy to Christ—then there would be no problems! It is the rebellion against living in the real world on the basis of who I am that brings the devastation.

Now of course sin entered the world at the fall, and people have been twisted and spoiled ever since. No one is fully developed into what or who he or she could be, nor is anyone completely fulfilled. That will not exist until we have our new bodies at the return of Christ and all the shattered creation is restored. However, to turn away from what God has set forth as the basic rules of how to live in the light of what He has created is to turn away from any possibility of having a fraction of restoration in this life.

CHAPTER TEN

The First Apartment

Settled down in our first apartment, we made our own furniture out of a variety of old things, but the place was so small it didn't need much. Fran scraped the old paint from the dressing table, the chest of drawers, and the three-quarter size iron bed that had been his at home. Repainted in a cream color and given new drawer handles fashioned of London tan leather, those pieces of furniture, along with the new curtains and bedspread of brown and white, transformed the tiny room into a really lovely looking place. It didn't matter that a card table for study had no room; it could rest on the bed, with two feet on the floor, and Fran was all set for night-after-night seminary "swatting." I set up the sewing machine and my leather work in the tiny living room. There were brown, white, and yellow laced-together leather covers on the couch which Fran had made from the old springs, and the cedar chest was covered with turquoise pique I had "picked up" in Philadelphia's South Fourth Street, along with the material for the curtains, bedspread, and pillows. It was all uncomfortable but elegant, with Mother and Dad's old straight chairs of no "period" sanded and covered (that is, the seats) with more of the cream-colored leather.

We had chosen a White's Domestic cabinet sewing machine rather than the similar Singer, simply to save $13.95 . . . which was enough to buy the gate-leg table, which when pulled out would serve our seminary dinner guests! That sewing machine, along with the leather and two punches, was to provide our living during the depression's lack of jobs. Yes, I was a working wife. It didn't seem to be a subject of conversation or of question. It seemed the perfectly normal thing to do when one's husband was working on studies essential to whatever the future would be for both of us. My creativity was having an opening, and ingenuity was also, but these reasons didn't have to be given. The topic wasn't on people's lips. Anyway, my mother had been a working mother as a China Inland Mission missionary, along with all the other mothers and wives.

It seemed to me that a woman's "place" was to share the life and the work of the man she had made a choice to say "yes" to in whatever way the moment of history required, with the possibilities and diversities being endless. Farmers and their wives share the haying or the freezing of corn. The scope of going through life shoulder to shoulder in work, home, and vacation, includes a variety of changing "roles"—if you want to use that word, which I don't like. So I did dressmaking, and I designed, made and sold leather belts and buttons. The proceeds went to purchase our food and gas and so on—just enough to squeak through.

Fran shared in a weekly thorough housecleaning in which we polished everything, washed windows, shook out our little rag rugs, washed and waxed floors, and so on. We had no vacuum cleaner, or even rugs to vacuum. He also helped with the washing, plunging a contraption on the end of a broomstick into the sheets and towels and other items as they soaked in a soapy water in the bathtub. Long wringing and rinsing followed, and we hauled the various items out to the tin roof to hang them up on the inevitable lines out there. A homey feeling. Fran had taken two butter tubs and filled them with wonderful dirt from the Wissahickon woods, and by the next spring we were growing a lush crop of heavenly blue morning glories as well as petunias, ivy, and some ageratum. Our garden turned that ugly roof into a penthouse roof garden as far as we were concerned.

The home should be a place where creativity is encouraged and appreciated. A clean and orderly house is a joy to everyone, yet there is a need to be sensitive to the greater importance of creativity.

CHAPTER ELEVEN

Inspiring Creativity in the Home

God created. The Personal God who has always existed has always been creative. The evidence of His creativity we are able to see, day by day, all of our lives. We did not hear His stars which sang together eons of time ago, but we do hear the variety of notes in bird songs in almost original beauty in woods, jungles, along lake shores and mountain streams, and then we hear them copied in wind and string instruments. We have never seen His unspoiled planets and stars, moon and sun, mountains and seas, flowers and trees. But the leftover beauty which we do have in these creations of God is all that our own spoiled nervous system can stand.

God also made man in His own image, with the capacity to create, and also the capacity to enjoy and respond to Creation—God's Creation—and the creations of other human beings. The family should be the place where the wife's, husband's and child's creativity is encouraged and appreciated.

An atmosphere of two-way communication, which involves listening as well as talking, and taking an interest in the other person's thoughts and ideas is needed if creativity is to be encouraged. A mutual trust is built up in carefully listening to even the wildest and the most impossible-sounding projects. If the response is always, "Oh, that's impossible," then the communication doesn't continue. A person gets discouraged in setting forth an idea if it is immediately ruled out.

An atmosphere of trust brings forth a sharing of ideas and an attempt to make things, with an expectation that the most wonderful thing is just about to come forth. This atmosphere comes if the basic attitude is one which takes mistakes and fresh attempts as quite expected.

An atmosphere conducive to creativity must be one of respect for the young (or old) artist—however talented or clumsy the attempt has been. Creativity needs the availability of reaching the attention of a sympathetic friend at just the right moment. This is true in the budding of creativity in an early childhood moment, but it is just as true in the serious creativity of a genius. Someone needs to come and watch, listen, look, respond. If there is helpful criticism to be given, the first flush of excited completion of a work is not the moment to give it.

All too often, when a baby takes its first step, there is a burst of laughter that practically knocks him down, and fear to try again hinders for a length of time. This can be true of any first step in cooking, gardening, drawing, carpentry work, making a mud pie, playing a piano or recorder, making a rag doll, sewing, making a lamp or whatever. Whether it is a tiny child's first creative effort or an adult's timid beginning of something new, that first step can be turned into a full stop because of the very wrong kind of reaction on the part of others.

A good rule to remember (whether you are dealing with a three-year-old person, a thirty-three-year-old, or a sixty-three-year-old) is that right after the baby song, play, picture has been presented, right after the mature painting, lecture, music has been introduced, right after you have read the most important book chapter, heard the sermon, listened to the cello solo, looked at the statue—anything you say must be positive. The human being looking for understanding needs to find it at this moment. The need for sharing what has been exciting in bringing this forth—whatever this is—needs response. The spark must meet another spark, or the fire dies out and dark discouragement can flood in.

Discussion, constructive criticism, presentation of some thoughts on what has been done, cannot be given to anyone at the wrong moment. The right moment comes later.

And remember, if creative projects are to follow one after another, there must be a balance in priorities. A clean and orderly house is a joy to everyone, yet there is a need to be sensitive to the greater importance of freedom to paint, mix clay, scatter pieces of cloth in cutting out a dress or a sail. The possibility of getting soil on a waxed floor is suddenly far less important.

Creativity can be a way of expressing love within the family. Don't just say, "I love you." Make something with love all sewn up in it or painted on it or arranged in flower patterns! Beauty should be important as an inspiration to doing the best with what is at hand for the Christian family. As much as possible, each new family should prepare a home with as much to inspire as possible.

Criticism of each other may be very necessary at times,

but there must be encouraged sensitivity to

the fact that the whole point of communication is to

have a growing relationship come forth.

CHAPTER TWELVE

The Balance of Differences

It's the balance that counts all through life. It's the balance that matters in the Christian life. It's the balance that matters in human relationships. It's the balance that matters in family life. There is a delicate balance, like the equal weight of two people seesawing, or like someone walking a tightrope. Too much on one side, too much on the other, and there comes the thud of one person on the seesaw or the fall of the person on the rope—the continuity of what was going on comes to a sudden stop. Balance is the very important ingredient in every area of life.

God made man and woman. The first balance that was given was before sin entered into the relationship, a perfect balance of two being one, spiritually, intellectually and physically. All the imbalances have come as a result of sin upsetting the perfect balance. Anytime there is any "danger" (in Satan's way of looking at it) of anything having a possibility of being back in balance, Satan, of course, would strike out to destroy that balance.

One of the most clever blows to the existence of the family is the attempt to destroy the antithesis of male and female as different, but fulfilling each other and having the possibility of being one, with the added possibility of bringing forth new human beings who are a blend of the two. The blow against enhancing and enjoying the differences between men and women and making it a "dirty word" to say that there are differences is a blow against one of the most beautiful and delicate of all balances.

What is being done to men and women is to push one "up in the air" with the other one "down on the ground," with Satan's foot planted on the end of the seesaw, so to speak! Satan is laughing his head off at the struggle to get free from his foot. He watches amused as Christians as well as non-Christians fall into the confusion of the declaration he sets forth in a flood of books, papers, magazines, movies, lectures—all saying that there is no male-female difference, and that there must not be. Poor, trembling people on top of the seesaw, hair blowing in the breeze, fearful as the breeze whips into a wind, not knowing how to get down! People are "up in the air" because of the lack of balance in anything they have been taught, and struggling not to recognize what they feel inside of themselves—struggling against the feminineness of being a woman, struggling against the masculineness of being a man, trying to feel neuter. The unfair weight is being put on by a clever intelligence who can slip out of sight!

As Christian couples and parents we have a responsibility to help in keeping very clear the beauty of the balance of differences. Marvelous to have a father who is a rock, a strong tower, a defense against attack, a counselor, a shelter against enemies. Wonderful to have a mother who is able to concentrate on teaching, being sensitive to the child's needs, compassionate and warm and cuddly and providing the atmosphere of home in the very way of serving food, of making clothing, of doing some of those things pointed out in Proverbs 31. Wonderful to have communication with both parents contributing, in agreement, yet with slightly different angles of understanding. What a need there is for teaching little boys that it is great to be a boy "because you will be a father and love and care for children of your own." What a need for teaching little girls that it is wonderful to be a mother "because you can bring forth a baby that will grow in your own body, and feed at your breast."—"No, the father can't feed the baby at his breast, and no, he can't bring it forth out of his body after nine months of growing there, because God made man and woman to have different parts in the matter of being parents."— "Yes, the baby is half of each person because the seed is planted by the father and is as much a part of him as of the mother. While the father is doing other things to get the home ready for the baby and preparing wonderful things for the baby to enjoy, and ways the baby can learn, the mother is free to have the baby right inside her, and have that be one of the very important things she can do." There is a balance—men and women.

Day-by-day living in the midst of an outpouring of

examples of love is needed through months

and years, if love is to be a basic part of the

¨warp and woof¨ of a person.

CHAPTER THIRTEEN

Fran's First Pastorate

We were packing again. It had only been nine months since we had moved to Wilmington with two-month-old Priscilla. Now seminary graduation was over; it was still May; Priscilla was eleven months old and walking, to our great excitement; and the apartment was being dismantled, with newspapers coming into their own once more for wrapping dishes, protecting the clock, bunching in around pots and pans, and padding boxes for books. The map came off the wall with a few pangs of regret, for instead of going to some exotic-sounding place halfway around the world, we were soon going to be driving about 350 miles to Grove City, Pennsylvania. It was to be across the street, in a sense, rather than across the sea. But we had said, "Anywhere, Lord," and as far as we could know, this seemed His clear direction.

Two of our new elders were coming to drive our furniture and all our other belongings. We would follow in the Model A Ford which had lived an active life for seven years now. A coffee delivery truck drew up in front of the house, announcing Howe's Coffee Company, and Mr. Howe and Mr. Hall solemnly greeted us, "How do you do, Reverend and Mrs. Schaeffer." It didn't sound a bit like us, and I was tempted to look over my shoulder to see who might be standing behind us. We were to plunge into a new category which somehow drew an invisible, uncomfortable, separating line around us—"The Reverend and Mrs. Schaeffer." Ouch!

The Covenant Presbyterian Church consisted of eighteen people who had left the "big liberal Presbyterian Church" and were meeting in the American Legion Hall. Next door to this lodge hall was a square brick apartment building, with eight small apartments. The first-floor apartment (turn right when entering the front door) was to be ours. We had a living room, a dining room which became our bedroom, and one bedroom that we decided would be for Priscilla. It was dark, but at least off to one side the kitchen opened into what then was our bedroom, and we managed to eat in there most of the time. Our salary was to be exactly $100 a month. The rent of the apartment was $36 plus $1 per month for the incinerator, and with insurance at $18 a month, you can see there wasn't much leeway for unspecified spending. We allotted $5 a week for food, so the shopping had to coincide with the moment when prices came down on Saturdays for wilted vegetables, day-old bread, and so on. As we unpacked the boxes our now-walking eleven-month-old found one that had been parked on the bathroom floor, full of such things as Vicks Vapo-Rub, aspirin, toothbrushes and toothpaste, nail brush, and other such items. Quick as a flash she delightedly threw them all into the toilet and pulled the handle . . . flush . . . down . . . overflow. The apartment belonged to one of the other elders of the church whom we were yet to meet—and the circumstance of meeting was not exactly what we had planned. We had the added pleasure of meeting the local plumber that same day.

Sunday morning found us next door in the Legion Hall. Here we were discovering what had to be moved around and put in place to turn the upstairs hall, which had a lodge meeting in it until late the night before, into a "church." The eighteen people did not bring their children because of feeling they should still have the benefit of a larger Sunday School and their old friends. I sat a bit nervously with Priscilla—trying silently to amuse her without distracting "Reverend Schaeffer" as he preached his first sermon after being ordained!

And what about the pastor's wife? For me, I felt my very big responsibility (along with caring for Priscilla) was never to stop praying for Fran as he preached. I felt keenly that it was up to me to pray for the power of the Holy Spirit, for the Lord's words to be given, for the message to really touch not only others but the speaker himself. "Speak to him, and through him" was not just a formula of prayer; it became the cry of my heart. This was to continue through the years, and it was very, very possible and practical for me to continue no matter what, even if we had just had a "fight" of some sort before he spoke . . . very possible and practical for me to "sit under the word of God" really forgetting anything personal, to listen to what was coming forth, and to be thankful that Fran was "hearing this," as well as to "hear it" myself. In the hope of helping some new, young pastor's wife, I would say that it is imperative never to sit thinking, "How can he say that when he has just been so unreasonable?" It is imperative really to believe God is able to speak through the one for whom we pray and is able to speak through us ourselves when we ask Him to, and at the same time to know that the speaker is being spoken to too. To feel that no one can preach who has not been perfect in the area in which he is preaching about, is to miss the reality of the truth of what fallen human beings are like, and what the Word of God is like. To grow, to strive for reality, to call out to the Lord for forgiveness, and to seek to live in the light of His word are of course important. But perfection is not to be reached in the land of the living, though we are called to teach a "perfect message" which has come from the perfect God.

CHAPTER FOURTEEN

True Love

Too often Christians are given false expectations.

"If only you would become a believer, a true Christian, you will be happy!"

"If only you marry another Christian there will be no problems!"

"A Christian marriage will always be happy!"

The hard reality is that divorce is on the increase, for both Christians and non-Christians. Why? Because imperfect people sharing weeks, years, in sickness and health, richer, poorer, for better or worse is hard. It can't work unless one or both "ones" put the other first, serve without demanding, constantly putting into action love.

Day-by-day living in the midst of an outpouring of examples of love is needed through months and years, if love is to be a basic part of the "warp and woof" of a person. This is meant to take place in a family.

The reality of love we are meant to strive for in our family life is made clear in 1 Corinthians 13:4-8, the biblical explanation of love.

"Love suffereth long, and is kind" (see v. 4).

Love suffereth long? There must be some circumstances during which love has to suffer a long time in order to be real love. That doesn't sound like roses and moonlight, perfume and soft music! What does it mean—"suffereth long"? I think this can be combined with "tribulation worketh patience" (see Romans 5:3), and must be understood as declaring that the circumstances which bring out the reality of love are not easy circumstances, but difficult ones. It is during the bearing of someone else's weaknesses and irritating qualities that love must suffer long, as well as in the bearing of the ups and downs of poor health, floods, fires and avalanches, poor cooking, and no jobs to be found! In the midst of circumstances which would not likely make romantic, airy, fairy emotions to fill a person's heart, real love suffers long and is kind.

"Love envieth not, love vaunteth not itself, is not puffed up. Love doth not behave itself unseemly, seeketh not her own, is not easily provoked, thinketh no evil, rejoiceth not in iniquity, but rejoiceth in the truth" (see 1 Corinthians 13:4-6).

Love isn't just a kind of soft feeling, a thrill of honeysuckle fragrance while being kissed on a June night. Love isn't just happiness in ideal situations with everything going according to daydreams of family life or married life or parent-child closeness and confidences. Love has work to do! Hard and self-sacrificial work—going on when it would be easy to be provoked and to think evil as the clock hands move, and the person hasn't yet come home. Love has to be preparing the atmosphere and words to make the twelve minutes left of lunch time pleasant minutes for the whole family! Love takes imagination and the balance of putting first things first.

"Love beareth all things, believeth all things, hopeth all things, endureth all things. Love never faileth" (see vv. 7, 8).

Husband-wife love, wife-husband love, and parent-child love—in times of weakness and failure, when forgiveness must be asked for and given, in times when suspicions have been right—love goes on. A child needs to grow up knowing that love never faileth, that not only will Dad and Mom stay together in spite of each of their weaknesses as well as strengths, but that the door will always be open, the "candle in the window" will never go out. Love doesn't say, "If you ever do that again, never come home." Love never faileth. Love keeps that door open, the light waiting, and dinner in the oven—for years.

The mark of Christian families should be the demonstration of love in the day-by-day, mundane circumstances of life, in the many moments of opportunity to show that love suffereth long.

The circumstances which bring out the reality of love are not easy circumstances, but difficult ones. It is during the bearing of someone else's weaknesses and irritating qualities that love must suffer long.

CHAPTER FIFTEEN

Fran's Search for Truth

In 1951 the Schaeffer family moved to Chalet Bijou above fields on the lower side of the village. This rambling old chalet had a hayloft and a stone trough of water outside where cattle used to drink or clothes used to be rinsed, and the rooms were heated by wood stoves. Hot water bottles and blankets were the "added heat," making typing or school work possible in rooms that froze water in the nights and took hours for the chill to be removed by small wood stoves. The stone stove in the living room held heat longer and made that the place where everyone gathered for special events and for all the daily "living" that could take place there.

The hayloft of Chalet Bijou, still full of hay being stored for the peasant owners, was the scene of one of the central "events" of Fran's life. He describes something of his struggles there in the preface of his book *True Spirituality*. Before we had left Chalet des Frenes he had said to me, "Edith, I really feel torn to pieces by the lack of reality, the lack of seeing the results the Bible talks about, which should be seen in the Lord's people. I'm not satisfied with myself. It seems that the only honest thing to do is to rethink, reexamine the whole matter of Christianity. Is it true? I need to go back to my agnosticism and start at the beginning." After we moved we had a lot of rain, and the hayloft became Fran's retreat. He would pace up and down, inside, or since it also had a long balcony, he would often pace out there, up and down, the length of the house, under the eaves.

Pilgrim's Progress talks of the Slough of Despond, as well as Doubting Castle. Where was Fran? How long? It is impossible to analyze someone else's struggles for honesty and sincerity and uncertainty. It is foolish to try to copy other people, or to repeat another person's experience. Sometimes it is important for someone to walk among thorns and sharp rocks in order to post warnings, or to mark the trail with freshly painted hiking signs, indicating the best path around some hornet's nest or a precipitous cliff. It isn't necessary for everyone to set forth in the wilderness to mark his or her own trail if others have walked that way before!

The advantage of writing thirty years after the fact is that I can see something very startling now as I read hundreds of letters from people helped by the unshakable certainties Fran ended up with as he came out of that struggle to "blaze a trail" for himself, but with markings for others to follow more easily. As he says, "L'Abri would have not been possible without that time." If he hadn't had the "asbestos protection" of the honest answers to his own honest questions, he couldn't have coped with the blast of questions coming at him at times like a surge of heat from a steel furnace. He isn't giving things to other people that he has thought up as clever answers, in an academic way, for theoretical questions. He asked his own questions and discovered—and rediscovered—the answers in the Scriptures. A great deal of prayer is interspersed in his thinking—prayer asking for wisdom.

Was I so wise as to know this would be the result? No, of course not; I was scared. And when a wife or husband, a friend, a brother, sister, mother, father, son, or daughter is scared of the "searching" or the "struggle" or the "rethinking" of the other person, it is hard to know when to talk, and when simply to "intercede"—that is, to intercede by asking for God's help for the other person. It is as important to know when to keep quiet as to know when to speak clearly and courageously. Just keeping quiet can at times be the greatest work or activity of a whole period of time during which an "event" like this is going on! Surely not one of us has wisdom enough to know when to talk, and when to be quiet, without asking God for such wisdom—time after time. I can still hear the cowbells in the field in front of my little office window as I would stop typing, often during those days, open my Bible on the typewriter, and pray.

Fran came to the end of this time with firm conviction that indeed God is there, the Bible is true, the word "truth" applies to the whole scope of life, and that the Christian life can flow on into all areas of creativity, as well as into day-by-day living. I'll quote what Fran himself has said: "In going further, I saw something else which made a profound difference in my life. I searched through what the Bible said concerning reality as a Christian. Gradually I saw that the problem was that with all the teaching I had received as a Christian, I had heard little about what the Bible says about the meaning of the finished work of Christ for our present lives." He began to "feel" songs of praise, as well as to actually sing in his hayloft! One day he said to me, "Edith, I wonder what would happen to most churches and Christian work if we awakened tomorrow, and everything concerning the reality and work of the Holy Spirit, and everything concerning prayer, were removed from the Bible. I don't mean just ignored, but actually cut out—disappeared. I wonder how much difference it would make?"

We concluded it would not make much difference in many board meetings, committee meetings, decisions, and activities. From then on, my own prayer times became more central to each of the day's twenty-four hours! I made a private resolution that each day, whenever the time occurred, I would not read a newspaper, a book, a magazine, until I had first read whatever chapters I was planning to read in the Bible, and interspersed that reading with prayer. I read and prayed as a two-way conversation. Also I began to write to the Lord, simply as one would write a note to emphasize something to another person in a more concrete way than speaking. For me, it was a more vivid way of communicating. Although I had struggled in prayer during Fran's time of search, now, with thanksgiving for his conclusions, my resolve was to have more reality in my life, in behaving (privately, alone with the Lord) as if it mattered, as if it would make a difference in history, if I acted upon the admonitions to pray ". . . on all occasions with all kinds of prayers and requests."

CHAPTER SIXTEEN

Wholesome Speech

Some things must never be said, no matter how hot the argument, no matter how angry one becomes, no matter how far one goes in feeling, "I don't care how much I hurt him [or her]." Some things are too much of a "luxury" ever to say. Some things are too great a price to pay for the momentary satisfaction of cutting the other person down. Some things are like throwing indelible ink on a costly work of art, or smashing a priceless statue just to make a strong point in an argument. Saying certain things is an expense beyond all reason. This is true for man, woman and child. Proverbs says, "Every wise woman buildeth her house: but the foolish plucketh it down with her hands. . . In the mouth of the foolish is a rod of pride: but the lips of the wise shall preserve them" (14:1, 3).

What is it that can never be put into words, which can't be erased and forgotten? What is it that one can resolve and succeed never to say during the lifetime of relationship with one person? What is it that is like plucking your own house down, pulling your own family to pieces around your own ears, and creating a ruin of the most precious relationship? It is attacking the person in his or her most vulnerable, most sensitive, most insecure spot in life. It is pulling the rug out at a place where the other person felt there was a solid acceptance and understanding, without question. It is bringing up something from the other person's background which he has no control over and which carries with it painful memories of outsiders' lack of understanding. It is turning the one secure place in all of life into a suddenly exposed place of naked attack from which there is no place to run.

At some point in the beginning of a relationship, it is of tremendous importance to decide inside yourself just what things are really "out of bounds," and to declare to yourself that you will never resort to saying anything about: his or her big nose, deformities, lack of cultural or educational upbringing, and psychological fears or special weaknesses. Naturally it can't be too big a list, but there must be certain specific areas you rationally decide not to let "wild horses drag out of you!"

There should be family discussion about the centrality of growing relationships being more important than individual points one wants to get across. Criticism of each other may be very necessary at times, but there must be encouraged sensitivity to the fact that the whole point of communication is to have a growing relationship come forth. If criticism is degenerating into simply a power struggle, one needs to stop short and ask, "What is more important, our relationship as a whole, or convincing him or her that I'm right?" There can be a change of subject, an introduction of a pleasant thing such as reading or music or just listening to the other, a game or puzzle, or listening to the news together. Every discussion in which two people are differing does not need to continue to the bitter end!

It is possible. It is a restraint that you can inflict upon yourself. Have you ever broken ribs or badly bruised all the muscles in a severe fall directly on your rib cage? I have. It is amazing how suddenly controlled is my coughing. How gentle and limited in volume is my need to cough or sneeze, how controlled my burst of humor—a quiet laugh taking the place of an unlimited guffaw! Immediate pain sets a limit, and the knowledge that more pain is to follow gives strength to the power of control. The freedom to cough, sneeze and laugh becomes too luxurious a freedom, the cost is too great to indulge in it, except with firm limits! This is something of an illustration. We do set ourselves limits in a variety of things, even in areas that seem spontaneous. Say to yourselves, teach your children, "There are some things that are too costly to say, some things that are too great a luxury to use in sarcasm, some things that are too cleverly devastating to ever use in trying to get the better of someone. To win in the midst of saying that kind of thing, is to lose entirely. What rare and marvelous thing am I losing in order to win what little victory?"

There are issues, no matter how unpleasant, that need to be discussed. But even so, seemingly mundane facts about the physical body must also be taken into consideration. It is ridiculous for a man to come home and begin to deal with a very difficult problem with his wife when she is dead-tired, hot, disheveled and in need of some sort of break. Better to suggest, "Why don't you take ten minutes for a bath and change before we eat," and waiting to talk over serious problems until supper is over and he has helped with the dishes, the children are asleep, and there is a relaxed moment over a cup of coffee, tea, orange juice, or ginger ale. Then, sitting before the fire or in the cool of the garden, the problem can be discussed very differently.

The same is true for the wife. If she has some request that is going to be a shock financially, an announcement that a new roof is needed, the news that moles are in the garden, a bill that has come for the third time, she ought to know that the time to talk is not just when he has arrived, tired and hungry, cranky from low blood sugar, nervous from a long, hard day filled with a diverse number of problems. It doesn't matter whether he is a doctor, lawyer, evangelist, painter, producer, president, plumber, electrician, gardener, pastor, businessman, professor, congressman, mayor, grocery-store owner, fruit peddler or writer. Whatever his work is, the arrival moment is the time for some sort of comforting fulfillment of a physical need—a hot bath or shower, change of clothing into pajamas and robe or blue jeans and shirt, a glass of orange juice, dinner. It does not matter what, but some sort of putting off the day and putting on the home atmosphere. It is when the physical needs have been cared for that the time is ripe for talking over the disagreeable problem or for proposing the new thing.

CHAPTER SEVENTEEN

L'Abri

It was June 5, 1955 that Fran said, "Edith, I'm going to dictate a letter to the Board," and I sat down in our "church room" (not yet a living room) and took that cataclysmic letter. We had been asked what we were doing, with strong indication that it would not be acceptable for us to stay there and receive people simply as guests to ask questions. Also we had come to a conclusion that if we were going to set forth to answer honest questions with honest answers, we needed to balance that with continuing to live by faith in some practical fashion. We had been living by prayer in a very vivid way, trusting the Lord to show us literally hour by hour what to do, where to go, and to provide the means. Now we were sure it was not meant to be an experience for a few trial weeks, nor even for a few weeks of trial, but rather that it had been a beginning without our realizing it. We wrote to the mission board that day, resigning as of that date. Fran continued that we wished our salary to stop as of that month. We said we felt led to call our new work "L'Abri Fellowship" and to pray that the

Lord would send the people of His choice for us to help, and that He would also send sufficient money for the needs of our family and the work, from the people of His choice. It was scary to mail it!

All this in twelve days from the writing of the letter to the board, resigning! Yes, we had made the choice to resign. Yes, the name "L'Abri" was something that we had been using even in Champery as descriptive of our home. But we couldn't have been clever enough to organize all that fell into place so quickly as we started to pray for God to unfold His will, as well as to send the people of His choice to us, and to supply the material needs. We were asking one basic thing, that this work would be a demonstration of God's existence. We asked, first, that He would help us to answer honest questions with honest answers, that people might know of His existence in recognizing the truth of true truth; and second, that our living by prayer, and His answering in a diversity of areas, might also point lost people to His existence.

L'Abri had started! What were our "visions" or "expectations" or "goals"? Simply a desire to demonstrate the existence of God by our lives and our work. Had Fran become a "perfect" person now? Had his quick temper been conquered never to rear its head again? Would he never do anything in his own strength again, and perfectly live by prayer, moment by moment? Was I now going to have no faults? Would all my decisions, moment by moment, be the Lord's decisions? Would I really be "dead to self" all the time, and have no frustrations as I cooked, weeded gardens, and washed dishes for an endless stream of people? Had Fran an "outline" of the answers he was going to give? Did we have a sense of having "arrived"? No, a million times no. But, God is very patient and gentle with His children, as in a real measure (only He knows the ingredients of sincerity and honesty) they attempt to live in close communication with Him, asking for help, asking for strength, depending on His wisdom and power rather than on their own cleverness and zip!

We were asking for "reality"; we were to be overwhelmed by "reality"! We continued to live moment by moment, having things to be thankful for, things to rejoice about with excitement, things to regret and ask forgiveness for. We wept, we laughed, we thrilled, we agonized, we squealed with surprise at joys and tragedies. Reality is not a flat plateau.

I wrote a letter August 9, 1955, describing the first month of L'Abri. How I wish I could just clip it to this page for you! I wish you could read in detail about John Sandri's arrival with Karl Woodson, on the yellow bus—John, nineteen years old, who was to say, "I feel as if I were looking at a new world I never knew existed before. You know, I never ever heard the word 'sin' in my church, though I went every Sunday. I thought Christianity was a rosy glow that didn't make any sense." Karl had been two years in the army and had been in Summer Bible School in St. Louis. Only the Lord's sense of weaving could have brought Hurvey's brother that day, along with John, who was within two years to be marrying Priscilla. How was all this happening? Where? What difference would it ever make? Huemoz was not on the map. We were committed to staying in that chalet and praying for the Lord to bring His choice of people. A trickle that was steady, but not impressive as to numbers, came only to disperse, so far as we could see.

There was nothing to "join", we were simply praying that the Lord would bring people to be helped and then take them to the place where He would use them, rather than our trying to hold on to them. As a month went by, the arithmetic of the gifts that had come showed there was sufficient for food, utilities, seeds for the garden, the few bits of clothing the children needed, and our amount to put away for mortgage. That month's total amounted to about three hundred dollars. A special gift also came in for the urgent repairs and electrical work. It was a picture of what would be taking place through the years ahead—God had met the needs, but there was never to be a possibility of stopping praying. We have always needed, and still do need, to pray for the needed funds—for regular expenses, and then for guidance as to any repairs or, later, houses to be added or branches to be added. We found that praying for money for needs accomplishes two things—it repeatedly reminds us that God is able to answer in these areas, and it also opens the way to have assurance that He has answered a prayer for guidance by supplying the money for a plane ticket, a boat crossing, a second chalet, a new branch of L'Abri—whatever.

A little old chalet on the side of a mountain, on a winding narrow main road to a ski resort. A family of six—father and mother, an eighteen-year-old in the university nearby, a fourteen-year-old in bed with rheumatic fever, a ten-year-old now deciding to study Calvert Course at home, a three-year-old needing some special help for his leg partially paralyzed by polio. No church, or foundation, or "home board" behind them. No big list of people—just 350 at that time on the Family Letter list, and 27 people committed to the Lord to praying daily as The Praying Family. The ending of that August 9 Family Letter was this sentence: "Won't you continue to pray that the existence of God may be demonstrated here in every possible way—materially, spiritually, and with His plan bringing the right ones here at the right time for the need of each heart? Nothing is impossible with Him."

CHAPTER EIGHTEEN

God's Financial Plan for Your Family

What is a "good" standard of living? How much is "too much"? How little is "too little"? What are the necessities of life? What are the luxuries? Do both mother and father have to work full time to provide? To provide what? What is most needed—the "things" and the abundance of easy-to-fix dinners to eat in front of the numerous TVs, or a real home atmosphere which someone needs time to work at, and the home cooking which someone needs to have time to do? How can a family be a family economically, rather than being torn apart by the frantic acquiring of money which will bring in an acquired number of things or pile up a bank account?

Two people with two separate careers and living in one house, but infrequently together—with children who are more frequently cared for by other people than by their parents—have really not formed a family, and the economic things have become a kind of people-eating monster taking all the humanness out of the relationships.

If economic matters are pushing you apart, rather than drawing you together, spend some time thinking and praying about it. The moments of material need are opportunities for taking seriously the reality of prayer. "Call upon Me and I will answer you," says the Lord in every kind of situation. To only tighten one's belt, do with less, figure out ways of saving, ways of making things at home, ways of earning, and not to recognize that we are meant to ask for help from the Lord, is to fail to demonstrate the existence of God to any who are watching us. If we believe that God hears and cares about us, then we need to be interested in His solutions as we pray for His help. We need to pray "believing that He is, and that He is a rewarder of those who diligently seek Him" (see Hebrews 11:6). The family should pray together about the Lord's provision for vacations, clothing, a pair of roller skates, or a new car when the old one is broken. Children should be brought up not to consider praying for material things as a last resort, but as a natural part of life.

In asking for work, for ideas as to how to earn money, or in asking for the Lord to send money in some special way for the immediate need, it is important for each person to search his or her own heart as to the honesty in asking, "Are we each really wanting the Lord's will for us as a family?" Are we wanting His kind of work for us, His use of our lives, or have we put up limits and are we asking God to supply some work within those limits? Are we asking for what He knows we need? Or are we asking for far more than we need? Often He gives us far more than we need, but in seeking our motives and our willingness for what the Lord wants, it is easy to fall into asking amiss.

A family is an economic unit—willing to live in conditions "better and worse" in different times of life, expecting to have ideas and a pioneering spirit at times, but also having a deep understanding together that the family is not floating alone in an impersonal universe with no one to appeal to. We understand that God is there, and that the family members can, together as a unified group, come to Him and say with honest belief and expectation, "Please, God, do a new thing for us as a family, such as You speak of in Isaiah—make a way in the wilderness for us, and rivers in this desert" (see Isaiah 43:19).

The mark of Christian families should be the demonstration of love in the day-by-day, mundane circumstances of life, in the many moments of opportunity to show that love suffereth long.

CHAPTER NINETEEN

Faith for the Asking

I wish I had faith to pray for a house with the space we need, in the right location."

"I wish I had faith to pray for an apartment at a rent we could pay."

"I wish I had the faith to pray literally for food, as it is becoming a real problem these days."

"I wish I had faith to pray for the needs of my husband with expectancy."

"I wish I had faith to take God's promises about prayer literally in just some area of my life."

"I guess I just don't have the right kind of faith, because when I pray it seems like a recitation of words."

Is there some magic formula to be discovered for manufacturing "faith"? By whose definition has the word *faith* come to have a mystical twist, so that it conjures up a hushed atmosphere with sights, sounds and feelings enveloping the fortunate ones and driving out ordinary thought forms and logical understanding? Who has spread the idea that faith is separated from reason and mind—to be "experienced" even as people experience a light show with rock music, or a "spiritual" floating by means of some sort of chemical or plant substance which is swallowed or smoked? Is there a beginning place for exercising faith, as one would the muscles of the leg, when one is a Christian?

God speaks to us clearly concerning the base for faith, and the primary exercise for our faith: "So then faith cometh by hearing, and hearing by the word of God" (Romans 10:17).

Hearing has to do with physical ears, first of all—but with the mind simultaneously. Hearing is accompanied by some sort of action in our minds. Ears and mind are simultaneously involved. The Word of God is the Bible. What makes it different is that it is what God has revealed to man and is therefore true truth. It is not a floating, mystical, spiritual kind of "feeling," which bypasses language as it is normally used. The Word of God is truth unfolded through a succession of meaningful words written or spoken in human language.

When God's Word is expressed, there is a trustworthy, perfectly just and holy Person verbalizing something that can be depended upon. It is something to "hear" with the eyes, enabling us to speak the words inside our own heads and think about them, or to hear as someone reads it to us. As we hear, we are to be shaken with the realization that we are not reading something another human being has said, so that we have a right to our opinion. We are to be listening with a different kind of awareness, ready to believe what is being said.

God's definition of "faith" is to be learned with the same equipment with which God has created us to learn arithmetic and spelling, or how to bake a cake, plant a garden or build a house. Understanding does not come immediately and completely in the learning process in most areas of life. Understanding usually takes some amount of time, but the first requirement of understanding is hearing—listening and paying attention to the content of what is being said.

God tells us in Hebrews 11:3: "Through faith we understand that the worlds were framed by the word of God, so that things which are seen were not made of things which do appear."

What a staggering statement of fact, as well as a definition of where we are to start in our exercise of faith. We are forcibly thrust back to the beginning of the Bible: "In the beginning God created the heavens and the earth," and we are told to believe that the Living God has spoken the truth when He said He created the heavens and the earth. We are told to have faith demonstrated or exercised before God Himself and any others who know about it, by believing that God has spoken the truth when He said that He created all things.

It is the God of Creation in whom we are to have faith. It is His spoken Word we are to believe when He tells us He created the universe. It is our faith that the Creation actually took place which is to be a foundation for having the faith to "ask."

"Through faith we understand that the worlds were framed by the word of God. . . ."

Let us cast ourselves on our faces in the midst of twentieth-century discussion, and cry out for a reality of that faith to be such as will be pleasing to God. He has clearly given us the starting place. It is His definition of faith.

CHAPTER TWENTY

Death Parts the Schaeffers

It was to be forty-eight years, ten months, and one week after that July 6 wedding in 1935 that death was to part Francis and Edith. On May 15, 1984, as the grandfather clock struck four, and the Neuchatel clock echoed with a higher note a few moments later, Fran literally breathed his last breath and was immediately absent from his body, absent from Edith, and absent from two daughters sitting with him in the firelight and candlelight of the beauty of that room. Where had he gone? There had been such clear communication such a short time before. How can anyone say death is natural? The natural thing is to have a person be a whole person. The silent body, the unmoving body, the unbreathing lungs are unnatural to family members who have just felt a pressure of the hand (pressure commanded by a brain), who have just heard a communication verbalized (also by a living brain) so short a time before. Death is a part of death. Death is abnormal to a living person; it is not a part of life.

Cancer had been discovered more than five and a half years before. The leaves were a bright yellow that October day in Rochester, Minnesota—too cheerful, too beautiful—as Fran came down from the operating room where the node had been cut from his neck and the news had been given to him within minutes: "malignant." It seemed that the trees outside should have turned gray. Further test results and the program of chemotherapy were outlined carefully and with compassion by Dr. Monty Petitt on the afternoon of October 11, 1978. The next chapter of our life together was to be in and out of Rochester's Mayo Clinic with a succession of checkups and a continued program of chemotherapy to which I added a careful program of nutrition, hoping it would help his system handle the chemotherapy.

During Easter 1984 I was faced with a decision. "He is dying of the advancing cancer. Do you want him to be placed in intensive care on machines? Now is the time to make the choice." With six doctors bending over me with expressions that were not unkind, waiting for me to speak, my mind played back snatches of the many conversations Fran and I had had concerning the difference between prolonging life at any cost or prolonging death. "You men have already done great things during these last years and these last few weeks. You fought for life and gave Fran time to complete an amazing amount of work, including writing this last book and making this last seminar tour. Thank you. Now, however, if I understand correctly, you are talking about making a choice between having his last period of time being one separated from me and from all he would love to hear and see, or being with me and in the home nearby with all his familiar things and his familiar music. I don't want him to be separated from us until he is separated from his body! You see, I believe God exists, though you may not. I believe with no shadow of doubt that when he is absent from his body, he will be present with the Lord. I don't want him to be absent from me, from his daughters, to be shut away in an intensive care unit for these last days. I want to take him home." The response was almost entirely one of deep relief on the doctors' part. They seemed to say, "We wish more people would care for their loved ones this way."

There were phone calls to make, home-nursing care to be arranged, a hospital bed and oxygen to be rented. The bed was placed on the ground floor to face windows opening to the view of a tree trunk where squirrels ran up and down, and a bird feeder hung. Tiny leaves were appearing on the trees, and the grass was getting green, but no flowers had appeared yet. Debby, Mary Jane, Mike, Greg, and others pitched in to make a sudden "garden" in plain view, with pots of red geraniums, boxes of petunias, and a log with an old fountain fastened to it. (A bronze head of a boy that had been brought with the things from Switzerland. Ivy hid the hose that brought water to flow from the boy's mouth.) The things Fran could view from that bed, inside and outside, brought glimpses of different periods of life. It was a homecoming from four stark white walls into firelight, candlelight, birds of all kinds coming to feed . . . and music.

Music flooded the room. One after another we played his favorite records. Beethoven's symphonies and sonatas, Bach, Schubert, Liszt, Chopin, Telemann, Mendelssohn, and Handel. Handel's *Messiah* was played from beginning to end several times in the next days. He loved the full volume with the words and music thundering through him:

"King of Kings, Lord of Lords, Hallelujah, Hallelujah." With Handel, Fran responded, "My Lord, My Master." So often he had told our children of Queen Victoria standing in her box at the Royal Albert Hall to give homage to her King.

What a contrast—Handel's music wonderfully played and beautifully sung—with the noises of a hospital. I was so deeply thankful that I had made the decision to cross the sea and to bring him "home" over here for his last days. How do you measure time? How do you measure importance? I've toyed with percentages—what percent of a married life was made up of cancer. But I needed no percentage to tell me deep within my being that it didn't matter what percent of forty-nine years together these ten days came to. It was impossible to tie a price tag to the value of these ten days of being surrounded by loving care, by beauty and life, by flavors, sights and smells that brought back special memories, by music, music, and more music, as well as by words speaking of certain hope.

For the family, the three of us there (keeping the others in close touch by phone), it was a satisfying thing to be able to share cups of tea, to put another log on the fire, to pray aloud when he said "pray," to read to him the words which bridged the gap with a promise of what is reality ahead. For us it was fantastic to recognize that music was not blotting out a future silence, but that music was really what is ahead. Music is a part of the future, so it was not unsuitable to have music to share as long as possible, until we too can share the future.

Nearly 3,000 years ago the prophet Isaiah wrote words that were quoted in 1 Corinthians: "Eye has not seen, nor ear heard, Nor have entered into the heart of man, the things which God has prepared for those who love Him" (1 Corinthians 2:9).

That is a promise of forever music that will be beyond the beauty of anything we have ever heard.

No, we were not having a false kind of time, we were not bolstering each other up with unreality. When Fran softly said, "Keep on . . . from strength to strength," it had meaning all right. It had meaning for us because he referred to Psalm 84 which he was too weak to quote in full, but which we could look up and read. He was pointing us to the continuity of the pilgrimage to be finished by each of us. How gorgeous it would have been to hear the sons of Korah singing that Psalm with an instrument of Gath accompanying them. "They go from strength to strength; Every one of them appears before God in Zion." It was exactly four o'clock, two clocks were striking, when Fran's last soft puff of breath was followed by silence. He was absent. Absent from his body. But God says to us in the Bible that there is both a departure and an arrival. There is a reality of arriving and being present with the Lord.

Silence? I believe there is a burst of music unheard in the room of departure, but brilliant in perfection in "the house of the Lord."

Family began coming. Plants, flowers, trees, telegrams, letters, phone calls, and people began pouring in. There was a letter from President Reagan to be exclaimed over and framed, and a cable from Sir Bernard Brain of the English Parliament and a deluge of comforting messages from all over the world.

The fifth episode of the film *Whatever Happened to the Human Race?* was a part of the funeral service held in John Marshall High School. It seemed fitting to let Fran speak that which he himself had said was the most satisfying message he had ever been able to give. So it was that Fran's standing on Mt. Sinai, his standing above the Jordan River as the Israeli troops marched by, his standing by the mountain watching Abraham and Isaac return after the glorious substitution of the ram, his sitting by the open tomb reading, and his walking into the sunset as the Sea of Galilee's waves splashed on the windblown shore were our view of him as he spoke that which had been so important throughout his adult life. His desire was that others might know the truth and come through the substitution of the Lamb of God and be with him in the house of the Lord forever.

"Till death do us part" is a parting as real as any boat departure with a space of water widening and the shore disappearing. Together has been replaced by alone.

CHAPTER TWENTY-ONE

Building a Museum of Memories

Your life together is meant to be a museum of memories—collections of carefully preserved memories. Day-by-day memories are being chosen for our museum. Someone in the family, at least one person, needs to be conscious that memories are important and that time can be made to have double value by recognizing that what is done today will be tomorrow's memory.

Memories don't need to be just a thing of chance collection, but can have some measure of planning. Of course, no one can plan an hour, a day, a week, a month, or a year without saying and meaning that, "Lord willing," we will do thus and so. With that being laid down as an accepted and understood condition, memories ought to be planned, memories ought to be chosen, memories ought to be put in the budget, memories ought to be recognized and given the proper amount of time, memories ought to be protected, memories ought not to be wasted, and memories ought to be passed down to the next generation.

How can memories be planned? First of all, as a new family starts, it is good to carry on old traditions and to start some new traditions of your own. What kind of traditions? Birthdays should be celebrated in some special way. Each family can have its own traditions woven into the remembering of a birthday. Perhaps everyone screams, "Happy Birthday!" first thing in the morning, or the birthday person is served breakfast in bed. Perhaps it is your tradition to wait and surprise the person later in the day with an afternoon party. Outdoors the party can be decorated with long streamers of crepe paper festooning in loops from trees to the birthday person's chair (or indoors from the tops of the curtains or lamps to the chair). The birthday chair can be made into a traditional "throne" each year, with flowers tied to it or ribbons adorning it, and the gifts placed on the table before it. Of course, there can be a variety of surprises and changes, but it is a lovely thing to choose one or two things to become a family tradition, and whatever else is done, always do that special thing as well, year after year. If there is some tradition that goes with the birthday in your family, you'll find that the very preparing and serving and putting out the things of tradition will bring along the memories of past birthdays and give a strength to the feeling of belonging which comes as people remember your special day.

There is discussion among Christians as to how Christmas should be celebrated and what sort of traditions should be handed down. It seems to me that God makes this clear to us in Romans 14:5, 6—which strongly says that there are some who place one day above another in importance, and that it is up to the individuals as to whether they regard certain days as special or not. There is room for individual differences, as long as we do what we do "unto the Lord" in the way we regard the day. If you think that Christmas should not be a family day of gift sharing and special feasting together, but a day of special worship and fasting, then that is up to you in your family setting. However, if you are not going to make Christmas a special day for the family, then you must choose another day of the year to be your special day.

One day a year should be this kind of carefully planned-for occasion. There is something about saying, "We always do this," which helps to keep the years together. Couples can establish the tradition of giving each other a rose to celebrate the day they met or became engaged—or some other outstanding date private to themselves. Children can be encouraged to start their own little traditions.

Memories ought to be put in the budget. This is a sentence to underline in red ink in your mind. How do you put memories in your budget? It involves a choice. You have a little fund in which you have tucked away bits of saving when you have economized, or when birthday presents have been given to you. You could get a rug or even a new winter coat with the money. Then you get a Music Festival program for the summer and fall, and notice that there is to be a concert that both you and your spouse would like. The question comes, "What is more important, the rug, a coat, or memories that will last a lifetime?" A choice has to be made. Memories must be consciously chosen or your family museum will be an empty, echoing building waiting for new acquisitions which you will never have time to acquire. This is because people are involved in the memories, and the togetherness only lasts a certain length of time. The together-as-a-family memories are limited as to "gathering time."

Some choices involve time, but no money. For instance, you are together as a couple on a business errand. The "efficient" thing to do is to take the first train back home—but actually there is an hour or two or three that you could choose to use in a different way. Perhaps you could take the boat back. It would take longer, but you would have a lifetime memory of the sunset on the lake, a cup of tea in the tearoom on the boat, the feeling of being far away from everything. What you have taken is three hours to cover a distance you could have covered in about a fifth of the time, because of schedules as well as the slower pace of the boat. Is it worth taking two or three extra hours, when you could "get all that done at home" or "at the office"? Upon what basis is your decision? This is the crucial place of understanding where many people are blind. Are you actually choosing between that "luxury" or "foolish romantic idea," rather than keeping on with your scheduled duty for two more hours? Remember that you are often choosing a memory for a lifetime.

A family should have a whole museum of carefully planned, generously budgeted and consciously chosen memories gathered through the years. If you wait "until you are older" or "for a more convenient time," the time of life—which is like a river flowing under a bridge—will all be gone, and the "right time" will have passed under the bridge along with the rest of time!

CHAPTER TWENTY-TWO

Memories That Teach

The museum of memories will have memories not planned, not chosen, and some of them will be good ones—and some will be of flare-ups, arguments, disappointments, as well as of sicknesses, accidents and tragedies. Some family "skeletons," however, can be memories which will help in the next generation's married lives. THINGS TO AVOID also belong in a collection of helpful memories.

My children will always remember my reaction to frustration or anger of a certain intensity. When my adrenaline flows, my reaction is to try to get more done in the next hours than any human being could do. My hands move faster, my whole body goes into high gear, and I speed up like a car passing the speed limits—the needle swerves and hits the highest point! What has set me off? Some criticism or disparaging remark: "Why haven't you done . . . ?"—whatever it might be. "What have you been doing all this time?" Rather than sensibly pointing out what has taken my time (and what has been accomplished), I react by zooming into high gear and for the next few hours doing ten times more than I should, whether it is washing windows, taking the curtains down to wash them, cleaning out cupboards, doing piles of washing and ironing, or whatever.

Is this good? No, undoubtedly not. But it is my weakness and becomes at times a family joke, and my children can remember moments of amazing accomplishments that had a very non-glorious or non-logical beginning. I can't know just what all the ingredients are—it doesn't always happen, of course, nor can anyone else guard against ever reacting that way—but the lesson of what has been seen of this particular skeleton has not only been some tense memories, but memories of frank talking and figuring out by the children what to avoid in their own lives.

At times Fran's anger caused him to feel like throwing something. There was an ivy plant which came over from Champery to Huemoz with us when we moved, and became the main plant on the coffee table in our bedroom. When a flare of temper would strike Fran like a cyclone, he'd lift up this red clay pot and heave the ivy on the floor. The floor was linoleum and the only damage done would be a scattered pile of dark brown earth mixed with bits of the clay-red pottery, and an ivy with its roots exposed lying somewhere on the floor. A broom, dustpan and brush, another pot brought up out of the woodshed, some extra dirt added to the old, maybe a shot of fertilizer, a pail of hot sudsy water and a cloth—and the room would be cleaner than before, the ivy repotted and back in its place! This ivy became a family joke. (For a few years it was not a joke to talk about in front of Daddy, but later he stopped being sensitive about it and it became part of the family's shared experience and conversation.) "You know, that ivy is the best ivy plant in the world. I guess that's because it gets repotted so often!"—"Hey, look at the ivy! That's a bigger pot this time, and it's growing like wildfire; must do it good to be thrown around!"—"What happened? Oh, just the ivy again." Yes, the ivy was thrown a number of times, but then the day arrived when it graduated to a lovely bracket on the wall. It had grown far too many long fronds to stay on the table, and Fran carefully put it up with pins to climb along the wall. Never has it been thrown since!

Your museum of memories will not all be made up of chosen memories. There will be both good and disturbing memories which will help your children to have a realistic understanding of human beings, of life in a fallen world where sin continues to spoil things, and of the fact that there can be a rebuilding after an "earthquake," and that it is worth it all to go back and make a new start.

Acknowledgments

This book would not have been possible without the herculean efforts of Stephen Griffith who envisioned and coordinated the project. Special thanks to Bonnie Church for scrupulous research and sensitive editing, to Steve Diggs for overall design, to Steve Rigell for typesetting and his own design touches and to the superior staff at Baker Book House for making certain everything came out right.